from the collection of

Ryan Braasch
~Christmas 1990~

FOSSIL • IGUANODON • 150,000,000 YEARS

DINOSAUR DANCES

by JANE YOLEN

illustrated by BRUCE DEGEN

G. P. Putnam's Sons New York

For my Centrum Students –
they know who they are – JY

For Holly who delights in dance – BD

Text copyright © 1990 by Jane Yolen. Illustrations copyright © 1990 by Bruce Degen.
G. P. Putnam's Sons, a division of The Putnam & Grosset Group,
200 Madison Avenue, New York, NY 10016. Published simultaneously in Canada.
Printed in Hong Kong by South China Printing Co. (1988) Ltd.
Book design by Golda Laurens.

Library of Congress Cataloging-in-Publication Data
Yolen, Jane. Dinosaur dances / by Jane Yolen ; illustrated by Bruce Degen. p. cm.
Summary : Seventeen whimsical poems featuring allosaurus,
stegosaurus, tyrannosaurus, and other dancing dinosaurs.
1. Dinosaurs – Juvenile poetry. 2. Children's poetry, American.
[1. Dinosaurs – Poetry. 2. Humorous poetry.]   I. Degen, Bruce, ill. II. Title.
PS3575.043D56 1989 811′.54 – dc 19 88–11661 CIP AC
ISBN 0-399-21629-4
1   3   5   7   9   10   8   6   4   2
First Impression

CONTENTS

DINOSAUR DANCES

When the lights went low
Over prehistoric plains,
And the music beat
In rhythm with the rains,
All the mud and ooze
Showed the scientists remains
Of a prehistoric party.

Here's Tyrannosaurus
Dancing on his toes.
Here is Stegosaurus
In a ballet pose.
And with airy pterodactyls
Anything goes
At a prehistoric party.

Brontosaurus sits
And waits this number out.
But here's Allosaurus
Doing "Twist and Shout."
And seven little coelurosaurs
Hopping all about
At the prehistoric party.

"Goodness gracious,
It's Cretaceous
Party time again!"

WHEN THE ALLOSAURUS

When the allosaurus
Does a rumba
Does she lumber?
Is she limber?
Does her partner
Tend to slumber?
Is the number
Fast or slow?

When the allosaurus
Does the tango
Does she tingle?
Does she dangle?
Does she mingle
With her bongos
In the Congo
Afterglow?

When the allosaurus
Does the polka
Does she poke her
Partner's popo,
Does she pick her
Dancing dandy
By his fierce
And beady stare?

When the allosaurus
Goes out dancing
Is romancing
Her intention
Or enhancing
Reputations
As the dinosaur
Astaire?

MS. A. HULAS

Have you ever seen
Ms. Allosaurus hula?
It's like watching continents
Go drifting by.

First she shakes the lower forty
With a vengeance.
Then she shifts and
Ocean waves are tidal high.

There are folk who swear
When Allosaurus hulas
Buildings shake and faint hearts break
And walls fall down.

She's a number even Richter scales
Can't measure.
Son, be careful when
Ms. A. comes into town.

Don't stand near whenever
Allosaurus hulas
If you value life and property
And limb.

For if you're on the dance floor
When she hulas
Then your chances for survival
Are real slim.

TYRANNOSAURUS

He strides onto the dance floor
Each and every weekend night
With his head slicked down with hair oil
And his suit a brilliant white.

He moves on with easy action
And the ankylosaurus swoons
When he hums falsetto descant
To the latest pop-rock tunes.

But though he chooses partners
From the milling dino crowd,
And though he asks their names or speaks
A word or two out loud,

He doesn't really see them,
And he doesn't really hear
Anything but pounding music
When he's in his dancing gear.

He's a solitary saurus
Who is good for just one thing –
Dino dancing for his mirror
Where he reigns, a lonely king.

TWO PTERODACTYLS

Two pterodactyls
Dancing in the moonlight,
Sliding through the night sky,
Slipping through the stars.

They think they're in heaven,
Dancing under moonlight,
Holding hands near Venus,
Kissing north of Mars.

Two pterodactyls
Winging through a fox-trot,
Soaring through a two-step,
Gliding through a waltz.

In the midst of dancing
Everything is heaven.
They forgive each other
All their everyday faults.

TWINKLE TOES TRICERATOPS

From the moment of her hatching
She was kicking up a leg.
Why, they say that she was even
Dancing deep inside the egg.

Her daddy called her Twinkle Toes
And showed her off to friends.
She would leap and twirl before them
And do very deep knee bends.

Applause would shake the countryside
And echo off the hills.
Her dancing entertained the troops
(And paid off Daddy's bills).

Where once she danced so quickly,
Now her pacing is quite slow.
Her bones are growing brittle
And her movements don't quite flow.

Her scales are getting grayer,
Time has blunted both her horns.
Her deep knee bends are shallower,
Her feet are full of corns.

But still she moves to music,
Any kind and any place.
And when old TT gets up to dance,
They always give her space.

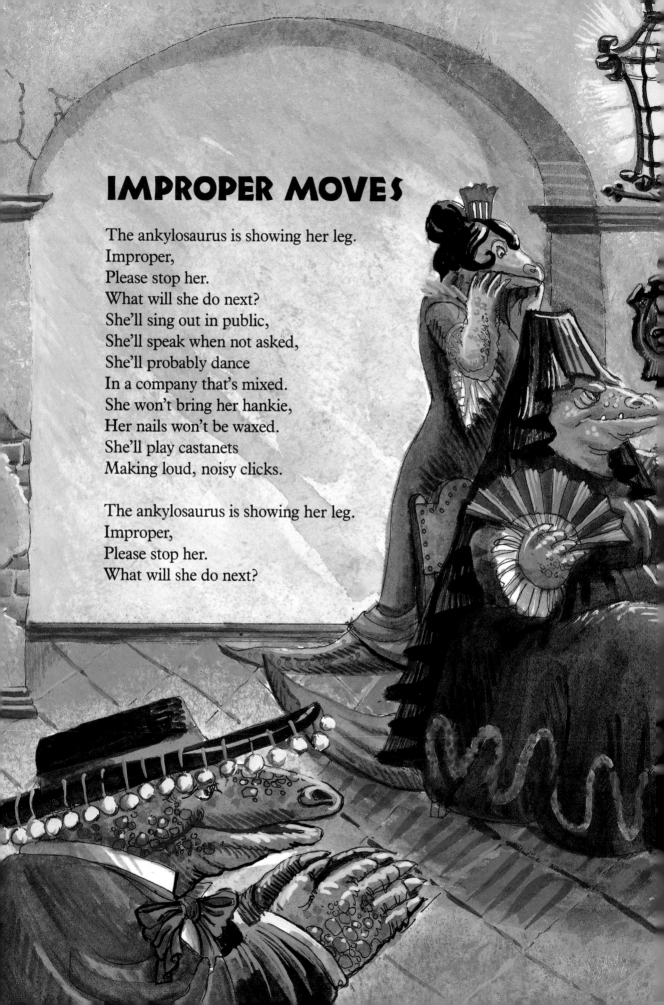

IMPROPER MOVES

The ankylosaurus is showing her leg.
Improper,
Please stop her.
What will she do next?
She'll sing out in public,
She'll speak when not asked,
She'll probably dance
In a company that's mixed.
She won't bring her hankie,
Her nails won't be waxed.
She'll play castanets
Making loud, noisy clicks.

The ankylosaurus is showing her leg.
Improper,
Please stop her.
What will she do next?

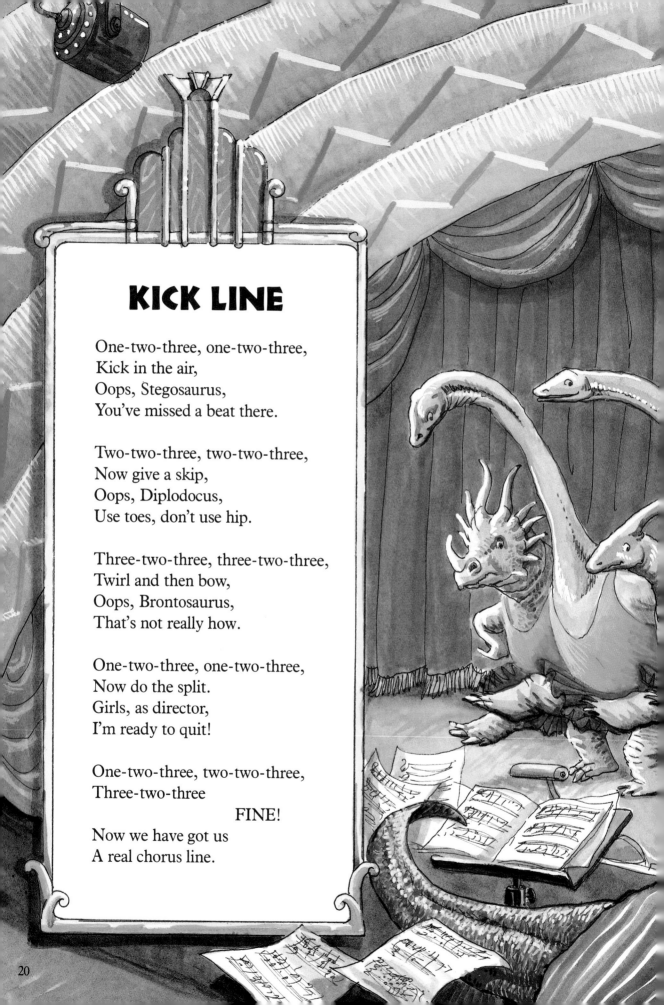

KICK LINE

One-two-three, one-two-three,
Kick in the air,
Oops, Stegosaurus,
You've missed a beat there.

Two-two-three, two-two-three,
Now give a skip,
Oops, Diplodocus,
Use toes, don't use hip.

Three-two-three, three-two-three,
Twirl and then bow,
Oops, Brontosaurus,
That's not really how.

One-two-three, one-two-three,
Now do the split.
Girls, as director,
I'm ready to quit!

One-two-three, two-two-three,
Three-two-three
                    FINE!
Now we have got us
A real chorus line.

DINOSAUR WALTZ

The lights are all lit
At the Dino café,
While overhead chandeliers
Shiver and sway.
And everyone knows
To get out of the way
When dinosaurs,
                    dinosaurs waltz.

The chairs are pushed back
And the tables are, too.
The pies put away
By the smart café crew.
The clock on the wall
Strikes a quarter to two
When dinosaurs,
                    dinosaurs waltz.

The music begins
With its one-two-three beat,
And then comes the sound
Of those dinosaur feet,
A rhythm that pounds
All the way down the street
When dinosaurs,
                    dinosaurs waltz.

One-two-three, one-two-three,
And there they go,
Whirling and twirling
And swirling just so,
Each dinosaur lass
With her dinosaur beau
When dinosaurs,
                    dinosaurs waltz.

I'll never forget
The first time I was there:
You wore a red rose
In your dinosaur hair,
And I would have kissed you,
But I didn't dare
When dinosaurs,
          dinosaurs waltz.

The music goes slow
And the music goes fast,
Just like dino love which,
Alas, does not last,
But leaves its imprint
On the stones of the past
When dinosaurs,
          dinosaurs waltz.

WALLFLOWER

No one asked Bronto,
No one asked Bronto,
No one asked Bronto
To get up and dance.

I know that she'd want to,
I know that she'd want to,
I know that she'd want to
If given the chance.

Why, she'd have gone pronto,
Why, she'd have gone pronto,
Why, she'd have gone pronto
Without more demands.

But no one asked Bronto,
No, no one asked Bronto,
Poor wallflower Bronto
Sat out every dance.

TOO CHOOSY

Here's Tyrannosaurus Rex
With his broad, developed pecs.

No!

Here comes clumsy Ankylosaurus.
If he talks he's sure to bore us.

No!

Look out! There's Iguanodon
With his red suspenders on.

No!

Don't look now, Diplodocus
Is starting on his way toward us.

No!

Here he comes, Joe Stegosaur.
Can you ask for something more?

No!

*Off they go and dancing free.
Is there someone left for me?*

NO!

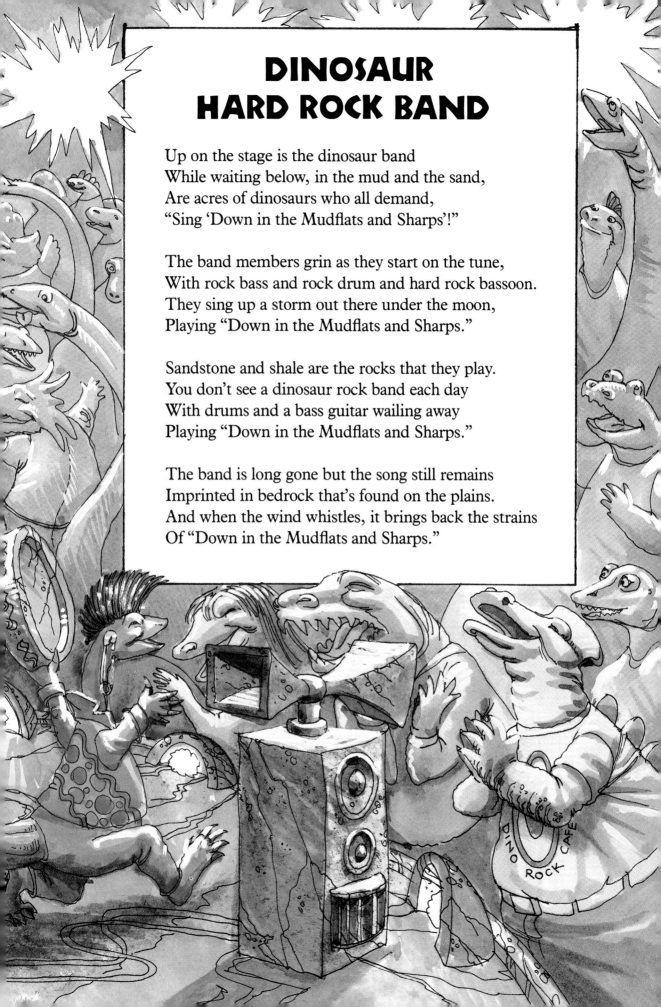

DINOSAUR
HARD ROCK BAND

Up on the stage is the dinosaur band
While waiting below, in the mud and the sand,
Are acres of dinosaurs who all demand,
"Sing 'Down in the Mudflats and Sharps'!"

The band members grin as they start on the tune,
With rock bass and rock drum and hard rock bassoon.
They sing up a storm out there under the moon,
Playing "Down in the Mudflats and Sharps."

Sandstone and shale are the rocks that they play.
You don't see a dinosaur rock band each day
With drums and a bass guitar wailing away
Playing "Down in the Mudflats and Sharps."

The band is long gone but the song still remains
Imprinted in bedrock that's found on the plains.
And when the wind whistles, it brings back the strains
Of "Down in the Mudflats and Sharps."

PARTNERS

Some dinosaurs dance lightly
And some simply clump about.
Some dinosaurs dance silently
While others hum or shout.
Some dinosaurs dance every dance
While others sit them out.

Some dinosaurs can do the twist
And some can do the waltz.
Some always mess the simplest step
While others have no faults.
Some take a soda at the break –
And some take smelling salts.

Some dinosaurs dance to the beat
And some – alas – do not.
And some of them tromp on your feet.
Some sweat when it is hot.
And some don't care if you are there –
And that's the one I've got!

31

DRESS CODE:
A SEDIMENTAL JOURNEY

Open the scrapbook and look at the past.
Dinosaur clothing was not meant to last,
Though dinosaur dance steps are carved deep in stones
Along with those wonderful dinosaur bones.

Dinosaur bones, dinosaur bones,
But never a bit about flesh or fleshtones,
Never a bit about dino dance clothes.
Yet what if we sat down and tried to suppose?

Suppose:

Some wore tuxedos and some tie and tails.
Some came in saris or covered with veils.
Some dressed in sandals while others wore boots.
Some put on tartans or breechclouts or suits.

Some dressed in ball gowns with deep plunging backs.
Some were more modest in blouses and slacks.
Some wore great surcoats while others wore smocks.
A few dressed themselves just to blend with the rocks.

The sediment shows us bare bones of the past
For costumes and clothing were not meant to last.
A fad is a fad. When it's done, it is done.
And second-hand fashion is never much fun.

A fad is a fad and designers all know
That once it is worn out, a dress has to go.
And that's why no clothes are imprinted on stones:
Only the remnants of dinosaur bones.

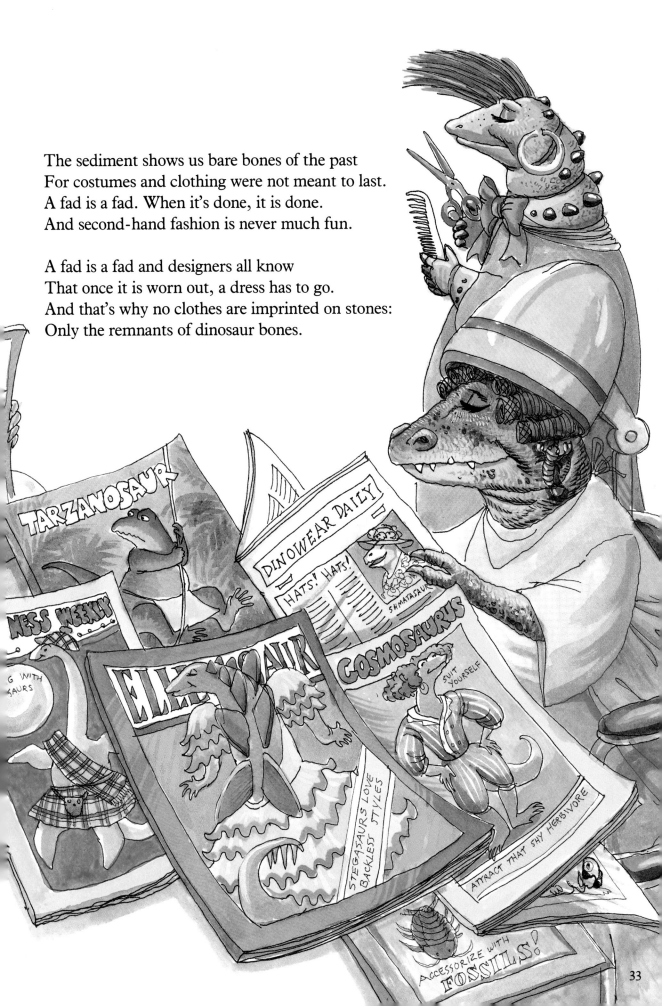

SQUARE DANCE

Swing your dino, dipsy-do,
Allemande and right on through,
Tooth and tail and bow and bend,
Greet the next saur as a friend.

> Swing 'em.

To the left and to the right,
Dinosaurs into the night.
To the music please attend,
Greet the next saur as a friend.

> Swing 'em.

Sandstone, limestone, mudstone, shale,
Fossilize and do not fail.
Leave your prints of front and end.
Greet the next saur as a friend.

> Swing 'em.

DISCO DINO DANCING

Disco dino dancing
Under bright and flashing lights,
A thousand thousand winking stars
In dark Cretaceous nights.

They swayed to all the measures
Of the prehistoric breeze
As it played its early music on
The Carboniferous trees.

We can only guess the time scheme,
We can only guess the tune
That the disco dancing dinos did
Beneath the mellow moon.

But it must have lent them energy
And heated up the blood
As they moved in ponderous rhythms
Through the soft Jurassic mud.

AND AFTER

The party is over,
The dancing is through.
My feet are all swollen.
And how about you?
The band is now packing.
Our footprints remain.
But they will be gone
In the very next rain.
We'll leave nothing here
From our sweet dancing night.
Not a hint, not a taste,
Not a print at the site.
And no one will know
How we swayed, how we twirled,
How we shook, how we wiggled,
Or waddled or whirled.
There will only be memories
Left in the mind
Of the great disco dancing
Of all dino kind.
But memories are better.
Our children will know.
They'll recall in their bones
How such dancing should go.
And late on a starry night
Under the moon
They will swing, they will sway
To their own disco tune.